GOD'S GIFT TO A MOTHER: THE DISREGARDED VOICE OF A CHILD

MOMMY, Why Are You Angry with Me?

(Misdirected Emotion)

Kimberly R. Lock
Illustrations by Matt Strieby
Edited by Rhonda Cotton

Copyright ©2014 Kimberly R. Lock. Illustrations copyright ©2014 Matt Strieby. All rights reserved. No part of this publication may be reproduced, distributed or transmitted in any form or by any means without the prior written permission of the author.

Mommy, Why Are You Angry with Me?: God's Gift to a Mother: the disregarded voice of a Child
Copyright © 2016 by Kimberly Lock. All rights reserved.

No part of this publication may be reproduced, stored in a retrieval system or transmitted in any way by any means, electronic, mechanical, photocopy, recording or otherwise without the prior permission of the author except as provided by USA copyright law.

This novel is a work of fiction. Names, descriptions, entities, and incidents included in the story are products of the author's imagination. Any resemblance to actual persons, events, and entities is entirely coincidental.

Published by KRL Publishing
Cover and interior design by Matt Strieby, Newleaf Design.
Illustrations copyright ©2014 Matt Strieby

Published in the United States of America ISBN: 978-1-949176-00-1
1. Juvenile Fiction / Social Issues / Physical & Emotional Abuse
2. Juvenile Fiction / Family / Parents
16.01.21

Introduction

Children are a gift from the Lord; they are a reward from him.
PSALM 127:3 (NLT)

Do you remember the emotion that overwhelmed you as you quickly and nervously tore the neatly wrapped paper from the toy you received at Christmas? How about the time when you received an unexpected gift from a spouse or family member? What about the emotion and memories you have when viewing the family heirloom that was passed on to you? How did you feel when you witnessed the gift of life? Regardless of the process (a wonderful nine-month experience or some sort of complication), when your eyes met the eyes of your baby boy or girl, you soon realized that the process was worth it.

Children accept our beliefs as truths because it is what we communicate and demonstrate as reality. Interestingly enough, our children do not belong to us. The Lord made us their caretakers. Why would God, who gave us such precious gifts, allow our children to look like us if they do not belong to us? Well, with the billions of people He has created, there would need to be some form of identification; however, it appears as if we as parents/ guardians have forgotten our responsibilities. In fact, children are often viewed as liabilities and not gifts.

Stories of neglect, abuse, abandonment, kidnappings, and even death, saturate news headlines of children from every age and ethnic group.

There are so many references to today's generation and the lack of respect (among other things); but we must return to the source and ask heart-felt question such as: Who is teaching them? In some cases, children are left to make adult decisions, acting on the behalf of an absent adult, all while trying to maintain their innocence as a child. Even in the presence of a parent, children are not given a voice to speak, often requested (more so told) to keep silent and not speak. Well, Jesus allowed the children to come to Him and did not forbid (or stop) them. Why is it that we, as parents/guardians, who God entrusted to be caretakers of His reward, give our time to these little voices?

This series of books were written based on feedback received from children between the ages of five to twelve (elementary schoolchildren) who have experienced some form of abuse in their life but were not given the chance to voice out or express their hurt and anguish. It was such a challenge to write these books because our children today are hurting. Instead of us determining the root cause of the hurt, the children are either blamed or ignored.

The early years in a child's life are critical because actions and words make a lasting impression and begin to form what a child accepts as morally correct (or incorrect).

It is my prayer that as mentors, confidants, parents, aunts, uncles, grandmothers, and granddads we will pay attention to the cries of our children. It could be the difference between life and death. Instead of dismissing allegations brought to us by a child, we should take the time to ask probing questions. As adults, we should be able to decipher between truth and false claims. If their stories are true, then we have just saved the innocence of a child. If they turn out to be false, then it is an opportunity to teach a lesson of the importance of being honest. In either case everyone wins!

The "Mommy" series is a six-book series consisting of the following titles:

Mommy, Why Are You Angry with Me? (Misdirected Emotion)

Mommy, Can You Come on My Field Trip with Me? (Quality Time/Attention)

Mommy, He Touched Me and I Did Not Like It (Molestation)

Mommy, Why Don't You Hug Me Like You Hug My Sister? (Sibling Preference /Affection)

Mommy, Please Don't Leave Me! I Don't Like Staying Here (Abandonment)

Mommy, This Week Is My Parent-Teacher Conference. Will You Come? (Concern)

MOMMY, Why Are You Angry with Me?

(Misdirected Emotion)

Mommy, I feel sad when you yell at me.

Do you hate me?

Mommy, it seems as if you don't love me.

I'm sorry that I do not clean my room the way that you do it, but I do my best.

Sometimes I spill my drink or food when I'm eating, but I do not mean to.

Mommy, can I ask a question? Please do not get upset. Did your mommy get angry with you too and yell?

Please don't be angry with me.

Note to Parents

As parents, we carry a lot of responsibility. These responsibilities range from the demands of our jobs, spouses (if married), and from the everyday stresses of life. We must realize that children, regardless of how intuitive they are for their age, children are unable to explain themselves as we do or to comprehend misplaced emotions.

Consider yourself as an adult who is starting a new job. You ask questions to ensure you understand your obligations, right? Oftentimes, you ask more than once. So why should you deny your child the opportunity to ask a question, even if it means a constant reminder from you as the parent?

If your child is old enough to have chores, show them how to complete their chores. If the chore is done incompletely, reinforce and explain why the dishes must be washed and dried or why the clothing should be placed in the hamper and not left on the floor.

Do you remember the person who influenced you to make the right decisions when you were growing up? More than likely that person spoke softly and took time with you. You can remember their words as if they were spoken in your ear today. Therefore, why not create a lasting positive impression for your children as well?

Harsh words scar like deep cuts from an open wound. Kind words are as soothing as a long-awaited hot bath from a chaotic day.

Kind words are like honey - sweet to the soul and healthy for the body.
Proverbs 16:24 (NLT)

Acknowledgments

Lord, we thank you for entrusting us to be a caretaker of these little souls that came from our womb. I know that you are depending on us to instill in them God-fearing principles that we are learning or have learned when we were children.

We will forever be indebted to you for the undeserving mercy, grace, and incomparable love you have for us all and have shown us all.

To my husband and my five children. Thank you.

for believing in me and entrusting me enough to be an adequate wife and mother and to share in your life journey. I love you.

To the children across the world who show courage and strength in the midst of such hardships. You endure things that some adults would not be able to. Just know that God sees everything and He loves you. Please understand that the misfortunes in your life are not God's fault but those surrounding you who may have made some harsh decisions which have impacted your lives. Believe and know that you will prevail, and you will be happy.

To all the parents, mentors, adults, aunts, uncles, foster care parents, and concerned people of this world who make it their daily obligation to change the lives of children and who may need an extra push of support, a kind word, or assistance with their work in the restoration of children's innocence; this series of books and thoseto come are for you! To those whose recognition may be unnoticed, but their satisfaction is to see a smile on a child's face, these books are for you. Your work and labor is notin vain. You may not be known by name or receive the highest of accolades, but you are known by your deeds. May the Lord continue to give you the strength and financial resources as you fight through your own personal struggles and hide the tears to show strength on the behalf of children you interact with.

You are appreciated.

NOTES

God's Gift to a Mother: The Disregarded Voice of a Child
BOOK SERIES

TO ORDER, PLEASE VISIT:
krlpublishing.com

Mommy, Why Are You Angry with Me?
(Misdirected Emotion)

A book about a child who feels that her parent is angry with her because of the tone of the parent's voice and a parent whose attitude is aggressive.

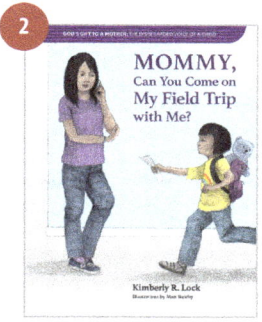

Mommy, Can You Come on My Field Trip with Me?
(Quality Time/Attention)

A book about a child who simply adores the parent and a parent who is trying to balance it all but is forgetting the simple things such as taking the time to chaperone on a school field trip.

Mommy, He Touched Me and I Did Not Like It.
(Molestation)

A book about a child who doesn't know how to verbally express being abused but knows that it wasn't the correct thing to do.

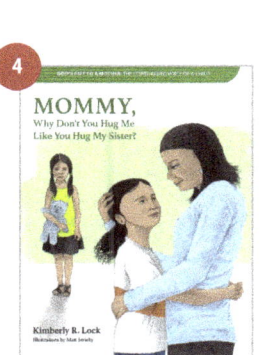

Mommy, Why Don't You Hug Me Like You Hug My Sister?
(Sibling Preference/Affection)

A book about a child who notices that the parent shows different emotion when interacting with her siblings and a parent whose children do not have the same dad and shows more concern toward the child whose dad the parent wanted to have a relationship with but didn't work out.

Mommy, Please Don't Leave Me! I Don't Like Staying Here.
(Abandonment)

A book about a child who may be left with a babysitter or friend but is uncomfortable with the surroundings and a parent who is trying to do what's needed to maintain employment and provide for the children.

Mommy, This Week is My Parent/Teacher Conference. Will You Come?
(Concern)

A book about a child who receives rewards and compliments of success from teachers but doesn't obtain the same encouragement from the parent and a parent who doesn't realize the importance of engaging in every aspect of the child's life.

www.ingramcontent.com/pod-product-compliance
Lightning Source LLC
Chambersburg PA
CBHW041322110526
44591CB00021B/2881